LEAD WHERE YOU ARE

CULTIVATING EMPLOYEE ENGAGEMENT
WHERE IT MATTERS MOST

KEN CARNES
RYAN CARNES

KEN CARNES AND RYAN CARNES

Lead Where You Are

Cultivating Employee Engagement Where It Matters Most

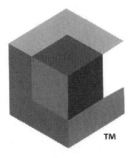

First published by Cornerstone Learning 2020

Copyright © 2020 by Ken Carnes and Ryan Carnes

All rights reserved. No part of this publication may be reproduced, stored or transmitted in any form or by any means, electronic, mechanical, photocopying, recording, scanning, or otherwise without written permission from the publisher. It is illegal to copy this book, post it to a website, or distribute it by any other means without permission.

Designations used by companies to distinguish their products are often claimed as trademarks. All brand names and product names used in this book and on its cover are trade names, service marks, trademarks and registered trademarks of their respective owners. The publishers and the book are not associated with any product or vendor mentioned in this book. None of the companies referenced within the book have endorsed the book.

First edition

Contents

Preface	iv
Leading Change	1
Leading Performance	19
Leading Relationships	38
Leading With Purpose	50
Leading Accountability	59
Conclusion	68
About the Author	72

Preface

Are you ready? No really, are you ready to step up and step in to leading where you are? There is an exciting evolution in organizational performance underway, with change and disruption impacting nearly every industry and organization. This evolution gives us a chance to reimagine organizational, team and personal performance and the impact each of us can and will have on that performance in the future.

For the last 25 to 30 years, organizations have begun to acknowledge that people are their greatest asset. However, organizations have also perceived their people as an asset that needs to be managed. Hence the position of manager and a process called "performance management" to manage people, their activities and results.

Thankfully, this is evolving. The successful organization of the future views their talent as a true competitive advantage to be enabled and cultivated, not an asset to be managed.

People no longer want or need to be managed, so the performance and leadership models of the past are rapidly becoming barriers to future success. It is well documented that a highly engaged and motivated employee population that is supported (not managed) by leaders and enabled by the organization produces more consistent, better bottom line results. This performance evolution is rapidly approaching. Are you prepared to participate or even lead this evolution right where you are?

This book was written to prepare you to thrive in this new and exciting performance environment. To help you proactively lead and pursue your personal performance, not have it managed and reviewed on an annual basis. To help you see the possibilities for change everywhere in this environment of disruption, rather than letting obstacles and barriers inhibit performance or simply waiting for change to happen and trying to react to it and manage it. To lead where you are is to find opportunities and ways to develop and cultivate real relationships in a world dominated by "bits and bytes" electronic communication, and where the art of the relationship is rapidly disappearing. It is finding a purpose in the work you do. Daily actions and activities that are purpose driven and not task directed and managed are far more rewarding and motivating. And it is to lead with personal accountability, even when those above you or around you might be focused on finding and placing blame or lacking in personal accountability.

By investing just a few minutes a day over the next week, you will be ready and prepared to lead right where you are, to make a positive and lasting impact and to thrive in this exciting performance evolution that is nearly upon us. Let's get started.

TO COMPETE AND THRIVE, EACH OF US MUST LEAD WHERE WE ARE, NO MATTER WHERE WE ARE.

1

Leading Change

"Change is the law of life and those who look only to the past or present are certain to miss the future." —John F. Kennedy

"Never doubt that a small group of thoughtful, concerned citizens can change the world. Indeed, it is the only thing that ever has."
— Margaret Mead

It is important to develop the skills and confidence to navigate change when it happens to us. In today's world, if people and organizations do not proactively engage in and lead change, they are passed up by the competition and often times cease to be relevant.

People and organizations that engage in and lead change, not just embrace it, but drive it as part of their competitive advantage, think differently and continually find ways to disrupt the status quo. They push beyond the bounds of comfort and safety and tend to thrive as long as they never lose their thirst for change.

Many organizations begin as market disrupters and change agents, coming out with new products or services that completely alter the way a certain market acts. However, if they are not constantly changing and adapting, complacency can lead to a downfall.

A QUICK GAME

Let's play a quick game of *Who Am I?* with two separate organizations. A description for each organization will be given and you try to guess the organization.

Descriptors for the first organization: VHS to DVD and video games. Failed to react to the digital age or even downsizing to drop boxes.

Descriptors for the second organization: Computer to laptop to handheld music player to world's best-selling cell phone and now on to streaming television and a payment system.

If you guessed Blockbuster Video for the first one you are correct! Blockbuster Video was a media giant in the 1990s and early 2000s. They dominated the VHS, DVD and even video game rental market both in the U.S. and abroad. With over 9,000 stores at its peak, surely it could withstand the test of time. Of course, as history has proven time and again, failure to adapt can bring down even the largest of companies. Blockbuster's failure to adapt to the growing digital market led to one of the largest downfalls in recent history.

On the other hand, Apple, while they struggled in the beginning to gain traction, has become a dominant force within the technology industry and became the world's first trillion-dollar company. From the Macintosh 128K to the latest iPhone, Apple has continued to adapt to the ever-changing technology market with new products and services.

There was a brief period where they struggled with new innovation, products began to get stale and sales started declining, however, with the release of the iPod in 2001, they unleashed the first stepping stone to what has become the world's most popular smart phone. From desktop computers, to personal laptop computers, to digital music devices, to cell phones and tablets, Apple is an excellent example of how leading change can propel an organization. And they continue to change, not resting on their laurels, but boldly and thoughtfully using their accomplishments as a foundation for their future.

INDUSTRY GAME-CHANGERS

Now let's look at a few more quick examples of organizations, new and old, that are currently gaining success through change and disruptive thinking:

As of early 2020, the largest personal transportation company in the world owns no vehicles. The largest accommodations organization owns very few buildings. And a legacy toy company that was on the brink of bankruptcy is now a leader once again.

What drives the success of Uber Technologies, AirBNB, and The Lego Group? An unwavering focus on leading change and productive disruption! These organizations have built foundations of adaptive change and do not let current markets or a "That's just the way things are!" mindset disrupt their focus on leading change within their respective industries.

LEADING OUR OWN CHANGE

Now, most of us do not work for these organizations and many of us are not even in positions of authority to directly impact top-down organizational change. What are we to do if the organization we work for is falling flat in this area? Just give up? Not at all! Even in situations where massive sweeping change is out of our control, we can still focus on the things we can control. We can control our ability to lead change every day from where we are. Leading change is not waiting for change, it is constantly looking for ways to challenge the status quo and intervening positively when things, even those things that may seem trivial, start to drift.

Admittedly, this is not always easy and it can be even harder for those who tend to resist change. But as with everything, once we start to do something over and over again, it becomes second nature.

THE FIVE LEADING CHANGE BEHAVIORS

To effectively lead change there are five steps that are key for us to enhance, develop, or modify.

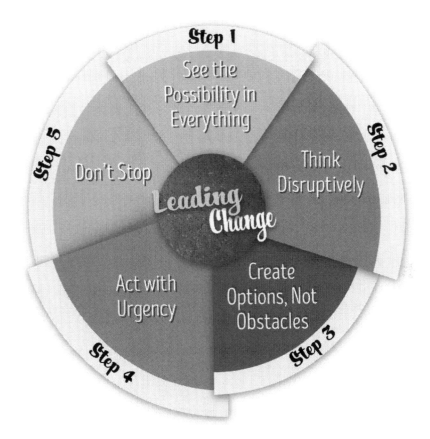

Leading Change Steps

See the Possibilities in Everything

All around us are possibilities for change. We often miss these opportunities because we are too busy trying to navigate the change happening to us, which ends up draining our energy and enthusiasm while creating a negative impact on our results.

Just sit and think for a moment of all the possibilities for change around you right now in both your personal and work life. These changes do not need to be anything monumental; sometimes small changes can make the biggest differences. When we are leading change, we are not sitting around waiting for things to happen to us, we are always thinking and imagining how we can challenge current and past thinking, actions and behaviors.

NARRATIVE CASE STUDY

Remember the Blockbuster example? They failed to adapt and see possibilities in their own industry. With large companies like Blockbuster and Hollywood Video going under, how is it possible a company named Family Video still has hundreds of locations with thousands of employees? As the sole-surviving video rental chain, how have they been able to keep their doors open? By seeing possibilities. For starters, they own their own real estate instead of renting, which has helped avoid poor lease negotiations. That is certainly a wise business decision, but that doesn't explain why people still keep coming into the stores to rent videos.

Customers keep coming in and keep renting videos because they have created a different atmosphere for the customer. The focus is on creating an experience for the customer when they walk in. The customers enjoy walking into the store because of the kid-friendly, "family movie night" atmosphere created. Family Video has also partnered with a pizza chain to open up locations right next door. You can call to order a pizza and a movie and have the delivery person deliver both right to your door. They also decided to purchase all their movies instead of participating in the standard revenue-sharing model, which allows them to keep all profits. In an industry where almost all of the competition has shut down, Family Video chose to see different possibilities.

THINK INCREMENTAL, NOT MONUMENTAL

As we said earlier, change does not have to be monumental. Small, incremental changes can be just as effective, and sometimes even more so. We have to remember that our focus should be on the things we can control, things like our attitude and behaviors, enhancing our relationships (more on this later), and looking for service and product enhancements for both our internal and external customers.

There truly is possibility in nearly every aspect of our lives and businesses. The key is to practice and cultivate your ability to recognize the change as an opportunity and not as a barrier or obstacle to our success.

> *"You've done it before and you can do it now. See the positive possibilities. Redirect the substantial energy of your frustration and turn it into positive, effective, unstoppable determination."*
> –Ralph Marston

Think Disruptively

Thinking disruptively is all about continually asking ourselves, "What is possible?". As we begin to see the possibilities in everything around us, our next step is to think about the what, why and how change needs to happen.

Have you ever been sitting at your desk and thought about how something around you could be better or more efficient? Well congratulations, you were seeing the possibilities. But then what happened? Probably nothing. The opportunity probably came and went without any additional thought as to how to make it possible. This is where most change efforts fail. People fall back into the mold of letting things happen to them and it is not hard to see why. Each day we are slammed with emails, requests, projects - the list goes on - and we put our thoughts to improve or change things on the back burner until eventually that flame burns out and we completely forget about it.

Once we transform the way we operate on a day-to-day basis and begin to make things happen instead of just letting them happen, our whole world begins to change. Those small, incremental changes can suddenly become monumental ones. Think on this for a moment. What would that monumental change look like? We have seen first-hand what this kind of thinking can achieve.

NARRATIVE CASE STUDY

The dreaded end of quarter close was here. Stress was high and morale low, with long days and hours ahead for the accounting department in this oil and gas exploration and production company. For each of the last seven years, it would take eight or more days to close the quarterly financials. During that time, endless questions would come from senior leadership trying to gain insight into the corporate results, putting even more pressure on the group.

Not once during those seven years did anyone ever ask the question, "Why does it take so long?" Everyone just complained and accepted the timeline as absolute. People in the department had resigned themselves to thinking that that was just the way it was and pressed on. Until one day a newly hired revenue accountant asked the question no one else did, "Why does it take so long to close the books here? I have seen it done in three days before, in even larger organizations." While it is not an industry-changing disruptive question or idea, it was an individual stepping up and leading where they are.

That simple inquiry set in motion a performance team to think about the closing process differently, to explore options and make recommendations on how to move from eight days to three days. Within

90 days, the quarterly closing process went from a painful, stressful, slow and arduous process, to a four-day, cross-functional team effort. Everyone took ownership of the results and took pride in the effort to make the organization better and more effective.

Senior leadership now had information nearly a week earlier than normal and could make more effective decisions and quicker adjustments that could positively impact the bottom line. Seeing possibilities beyond the status quo just by asking the question, "How much better can we be if we looked at this differently?" can lead to some incredible results. The team thought disruptively, then acted positively.

EXPANDING YOUR THINKING

Now let's jump back to a few example companies we mentioned at the beginning of this chapter: Uber and AirBNB. Uber took a transportation industry embedded in city governments and completely dominated by taxi companies with unions and flipped it on its head. They own no vehicles (although, they are still thinking disruptively and this could change in the future) and have created thousands of jobs. AirBNB took on the hotel industry and provided a whole new option for people traveling to different cities. This has been an eye-opening change in the hotel industry, forcing hotels to begin thinking disruptively within their own industry by making a shift to focus on the customer.

Now, what if you looked disruptively at your role, your processes, your products and services, your relationships, your department, your organization, and your career and expanded your thinking? What would you find? Think disruptively. What is possible? And what else is possible? And then again, what else?

Right now, and looking ahead to the future, your world should be full of endless possibilities. Expand your thinking to always think about what is possible and disrupt past thought processes and the status quo.

The landscape is littered with organizations and people with tremendous ideas and great change initiatives that just land on "Someday Island" where "someday" we will get to making change happen!

Create Options, Not Obstacles

Engaging and actively leading change is all about taking possibilities and opportunities and turning them into options and recommendations. While we don't want to limit the possibilities of our thinking, we do want to start exploring what success might look like and how it might be achieved.

Take a look at the following graphic chart and begin thinking of the different opportunities around you.

	Control	Influence	Impacted
Near term		Significant	Critical
Mid-term		Marginal	Significant
Long term		Minimal	Minor

LC-1

By using the chart, areas of opportunity or change can be categorized into separate groups based on the urgency of the change possibility. Once the possibility has been categorized, the next step is to determine the amount of control you have over it. Do you have complete control over the possibility? Or if you cannot control it, can you influence it? Or if you do not have control or influence over the possibility, are you impacted by it? In preparation, prior to acting upon the possibilities, it is important to prioritize them into these three levels of control: Control, Influence, and Impacted.

By categorizing and prioritizing the change possibilities, a picture begins to form and we can begin to sequence next steps to create change momentum.

As a side note, none of this means the other possibilities should be ignored or written off, or that you should stop thinking of where and how you can make a difference in those areas, just that by narrowing the focus the "Change Ball" is able to get rolling. A few small wins can start to turn into larger ones, which motivates others, and before you know it, monumental change is happening all around you.

In order to pave the best path to success in the short-term, your focus should initially be on those areas you can control. Your "Control" column (ref. LC-1). Focus on these opportunities and split them into categories of time: near term (30 days or less), mid-term (31-90 days), or long term (over 90 days). For the areas you can influence, categorize these by the amount of influence: significant, marginal, or minimal. And finally, for the opportunities that you are impacted by, prioritize these by the amount of impact they have: critical, significant, or minor.

With all the opportunities and possibilities prioritized, it is now time to act, and act with urgency!

Act with Urgency

The most difficult part of leading change is just getting started! It is easy to write possibilities down on a piece of paper and it's even easy to prioritize those possibilities. But as the busyness of our day-to-day environments begin to pull the attention away from our leading change efforts, it is also easy for us to put those efforts at the bottom of our task lists. The "urgent priorities" of the moment condition us to react to change and not to lead it.

In order to lead change and be the catalyst for making things happen, it is not enough just to act, we must act with **urgency**. Do not try to wait for the right time, just get started. Starting small and staying focused will create that critical positive momentum that is essential for the success of change efforts.

With the prioritized list of possibilities and your change targets identified, it takes clarity, alignment, and accountability to consistently deliver successful change.

The Common Success Theme

NARRATIVE CASE STUDY

Benjamin is a Customer Service Representative for a regional pool supply and pool servicing company and has been with the company in various positions for the past four years. Up until this time, each division of the company, pool supply and pool servicing, has largely operated separately. The pool supplies were sold from the retail locations and online. The servicing department, which operated out of each of the retail locations, received their routes and servicing locations each morning and then headed to each location with hardly any contact with the supply employees.

Before accepting the position of Customer Service Representative, Benjamin had had the rare experience of working for both the supply side and the servicing side of the company at different times over the previous four years. After about three months in his new position he noticed a trend of customers all having largely the same complaint. They had to come to the store to pick up chemicals (or order them online) even though they had a service tech coming to their homes on a monthly basis from the same store.

From his new vantage point of customer service, Benjamin was able to see a solvable issue that was not apparent to him when he was in either of the other two positions. He then put together a plan. Starting with clarity, Benjamin defined what the issue was, what success would look like when implemented, and why making a change was important. He saw that if the techs could bring the chemicals to the clients when they did their service calls, the customers would be happier, and it would create customer loyalty. Not only would they be servicing the customers, but they could also ensure that they would buy the chemicals from them as well. Once he gained the clarity, he was able to properly present his proposal to his superiors and achieve alignment throughout the company. He explained that this new service would align perfectly with the company's vision and values, as well as their prescribed purpose of providing customers with an "all-in-one pool service experience." Once Benjamin had clarity and alignment, it was time to create an environment of accountability between himself, his superiors, the servicing department and the pool supplies department. He brought in a few people from each department to form a team to help create the best and most seamless way possible to implement the new service. After about a month of working together, they came up with a solution involving all departments working together, got final approval from company management, and implemented the solution in all their locations over the next 45 days!

As you can see, none of this requires a formal leadership title or position to achieve success, just one person willing to act on an idea. So, do not wait, act now, and act with urgency!

As leaders of change, the headwinds are always strong. Most people want and talk about change, but when it comes to initiating any change very few are up for the challenge. Many start, but as soon as obstacles, barriers, and the fear of failure begins to set in, change slowly fades and the acceptance of the status quo returns. So how do you avoid what happens to so many?

Don't Stop

Change is hard! Almost everything tries to resist it and people are certainly no exception. This is not a short book telling you that if you follow these steps your change efforts will suddenly become easier. However, leading change and the continual work put into all the possibilities will absolutely be worth the effort.

It is imperative to persevere in the face of all the barriers and challenges that will attempt to thwart your efforts. We often refer to this as getting past "splat." Leading any change effort can often feel as though you are running and everything is going fine and then "splat", you hit a brick wall. So, you take off in a new direction and "splat" again, another brick wall. The majority of individuals and teams tend to give up after hitting the wall once or twice. They stop seeing the possibilities and begin seeing only the barriers and challenges, and consequently they never get past "splat". What if those individuals and teams just gave it one more try? What if your next try is the attempt that ultimately leads to success?

ENEMIES OF CHANGE

When obstacles arise, adjusting, adapting, or even changing the course of action might be in order. Reacting to these situations with resignation, resentment, or just surrendering, while it can be understandable, will not garner the desired success.

Here is a list of common *Enemies of Change* we might have to overcome:

1. Group think and expert think, where the thoughts of many, or the thoughts of one, can stymie a change effort
2. The burden of what we know — yesterday's successes and failures limit our thinking and actions
3. Expressing criticism freely and withholding praise
4. Too many projects or too large a project to start
5. Controlling everything too closely
6. Treating the identification of problems as signs of failure and discouraging identification of issues
7. Talking a lot about innovation or disruptive thinking but not actually engaging in action
8. Innovative ideas requiring several levels of management signatures to even get started
9. "Too busy to start"

It is obvious that there are many enemies of change that can easily derail change efforts, but the most devastating one of all is when we stop seeing the possibilities and only see the challenges. Thinking beyond today ceases and we stop asking the question "What's possible?". Instead of analyzing circumstances and seizing opportunities, we simply accept having things happen to us. While these traps are easy to fall into, not accepting the status quo and choosing to be a catalyst for change are so much more rewarding, not to mention the path to success!

What if Steve Jobs had given up on Apple after the Board of Directors fired him from his own company? Or if Howard Schultz had not reengaged and reinvented Starbucks when it began to lose its way? Or, what if Uber just decided to call it quits when city after city and taxi union after taxi union began to push back?

What will you do when a co-worker ignores your meeting request to talk about how you can more effectively work together? While finding the opportunities and ultimately achieving the desired success is tough, the answer to this question is easy...don't stop! Keep the energy and enthusiasm high!

While so few people accept the challenge of leading change, those who do it make things happen, think disruptively, create options, act with urgency, and most importantly, never quit. The rewards, both professionally and personally, are monumental.

AN ODE TO A TRUE AGENT OF LEADING CHANGE STEVE JOBS - APPLE

This is his speech about "Thinking Different".

> "Here's to the crazy ones. The misfits. The rebels. The trouble-makers. The round pegs in the square holes. The ones who see things differently. They're not fond of rules and they have no respect for the status quo. You can quote them, disagree with them, glorify them. About the only thing you can't do is ignore them, because they change things. They push the human race forward. While some may see them as crazy ones, we see genius. Because the people who are crazy enough to think they can change the world, are the ones who do."

LEADING CHANGE ACTION ITEMS

Look for opportunities for change in attitudes, behaviors, relationships, services and products. Remember, opportunities are everywhere.

Think disruptively without acting disruptively. Make things happen and expand options without being hindered by barriers or constraints.

Take possibilities and opportunities and turn them into options and recommendations, and then turn them into action and results.

Start small and stay focused. Act with urgency by gaining clarity and alignment and by showing true accountability.

Don't stop! Adjust, adapt, or change course, but don't stop! Always be leading change!

2

Leading Performance

"The distance between number one and number two is always a constant. If you want to improve the organization, you have to improve yourself and the organization gets pulled up with you"
—Indira Nooyi

"I can only control my own performance. If I do my best, then I can feel good at the end of the day." — Michael Phelps

---

Have you or anyone you have known been surprised by a year-end performance review? You work all year long thinking you were meeting or exceeding expectations only to find out one or two seemingly insignificant performance issues from Q1 have surfaced and become the entire focus of the review. Or maybe the entire year-end review has become just about what you've done lately? What if it was not this way? Today, in most organizations, there is almost no daily feedback given. No recognition of where your performance made a significant impact, where you proactively resolved issues or created positive connections with people. This is a major opportunity to transform outdated, ineffective performance management processes. So, we ask again, what if it was different?

THE EVOLUTION

There is an evolution happening in both organizational and individual performance where the accountability for performance resides with everyone in the organization, not a select few leaders. One where we assume primary, not secondary, accountability and ownership for our performance and contributions. In today's work environment no one wants to be managed, and it is now our opportunity to move from just reviewing performance to pursuing performance and from performance management to performance enablement. It is time for everyone to lead their performance!

THE PAST TO THE FUTURE

But let us take a step back for a moment. It will be much easier to get where we need to go if we know how we got where we are now. Our top-down, command and control model has been ingrained since World War II and the Industrial Age. The accountability and responsibility for setting goals, establishing expectations, measuring performance, determining training, and providing feedback resided solely with management. That model worked in a primarily domestic, industrial, manufacturing-based economy, but as globalization and technology continue to transform what we produce, how we produce, and where we produce, that model must change. The time from opportunity inception to decision implementation is now hours and days, not months and years. The successful models of the past have become barriers to the future.

THE TRUE MEASURE

The true measure of any organization and its people are the consistent results they deliver and how those results are achieved. It creates an opportunity to shift the old performance model to one where we are leading our own performance. It is your performance, your impact, and your career in your control. Shifting to proactively accepting more responsibility, actively pursuing personal and team performance, and taking control of performance activities and results may not completely eliminate surprises, but it certainly allows you to lead the conversation, control the development activities, and take more ownership of the results.

Making the shift to leading your own performance versus performance that is leader managed or just annually reviewed sounds great, but how do we get there? By proactively leading where you are and developing a personal blueprint for your personal performance actions and behaviors that are aligned to your team's and organization's culture, direction and priorities.

This blueprint starts with establishing a foundation of greater personal and organizational awareness. From there, you create a framework for focused development that assists in enhancing your professional eligibility, suitability and viability. Then, ongoing reinforcement and continual enhancements allow you to reach your full potential while increasing your organizational value and relevance.

Once the foundation, framework, and enhancements have been set, establishing an ongoing "performance connection" is the key to evolving and shifting the performance model from leader-directed, mid-year and end-of-year performance reviews to employee-led performance connections that pursue performance.

These regularly scheduled connections are designed to establish clarity and alignment to the department's and organization's purpose and priorities as well as establish personal accountability for goals, activities and behaviors through an environment that you create of constant feedback and development.

Your monthly performance connections will set the ongoing performance environment and feedback loop to personally grow and develop the skills and behaviors that lead to delivering consistent and sustainable top-tier results with no performance surprises. Your performance and your career are now in your control.

YOUR PERFORMANCE, YOUR CAREER, IN YOUR CONTROL: ESTABLISHING A BLUEPRINT

Setting the Blueprint Foundation

To begin leading performance, we must set a foundation by constantly creating and cultivating our personal awareness. Awareness creates responsibility and becomes a catalyst for change and action, which are the key elements for sustaining performance. If we create and gain greater organizational-, situational-, and self-awareness, our foundation for performance success is solid and provides support that you can build on.

Organizational Awareness

The performance foundation begins with enhancing and gaining greater organizational awareness, leading to a clear definition of personal success for you that is aligned to the purpose and values of your organization and team.

The goal of gaining greater organizational awareness is to clarify and align our daily actions, activities and behaviors with the departmental and organizational purpose, vision, mission, values and priorities. This clarity sets the foundation for you, not your leader, to set personal performance expectations that you own and are accountable for each month.

Let's begin your awareness building by answering these questions:

- What is the stated or assumed purpose of your organization and department?
- What is the mission and vision of your organization?
- What are the key short- and long-term priorities of the organization and your team?

- What are the values of your organization, either stated or observed?
- What are the key job or role responsibilities of your position?

(Check with HR to review your stated job description) Note: Often, job descriptions that are on record rarely reflect the actual work you do. This is a great opportunity to update your position job description to reflect current work activities and responsibilities.

Gaining clarity and alignment with your manager around these organizational and job function elements is critical to ensuring that you focus on the right activities that contribute maximum value and deliver the desired results in the right way.

So how organizationally and job-role aware are you? Are you focused on the things that can lead to you delivering maximum results?

Situational Awareness

Studies have shown 80 to 85 percent of performance success is behavioral in nature. We can have all the knowledge and experience in the world, but if our behavior and interactions are not positive and aligned with the organization's values in all situations, we can negatively impact others and our overall performance. For example, have you ever been around a person who is negative about everything, all the time? Their impact is immediate and often far reaching.

We define ourselves by our actions and behavior, but we are judged by others based on our reactions!

Each of us responds differently as positive and negative situations arise in our lives. The response provided in these situations will have a major effect on the outcome and impact you have. For the most part, we tend to act with diplomacy, understanding and tact; however, add stress or pressure to a situation and all bets are off. We can display any number of adverse behaviors such as defensive, harsh, dominating, dogmatic, and the list goes on.

When we flip into these kind of reactions, it typically diminishes our impact and can have lasting and far reaching negative effects on our relationships.

It is important to gain a greater understanding of your situational behavior traits and acknowledge the impact you have when you react. For instance, when conflict arises is your initial reaction to:

Avoid it?

Confront it?

Compromise?

Collaborate?

Each one of these reactions to conflict will have a different impact depending on the situation. And each of us has a natural conflict style we gravitate to when these situations arise. Gaining awareness of, and acknowledging the impact you have based on your natural reaction to conflict, and then modifying your behavior, when necessary, is the key to gaining a more positive result.

Gaining greater situational awareness can give us the chance to modify our reactions in those times of pressure and enhance our ability to gain influence, trust and respect. It allows us to effectively lead where we are in that moment. You increase your ability to perform with clarity and objectivity and gain the support and help of those around you.

Self-Awareness

Self-awareness is the acknowledgement and understanding of your current strengths, weaknesses, tendencies and talents. In fact, enhancing your situational awareness relies on your ability to have keen self-awareness. The more self-aware you are, the more you understand what impact, both positive and negative, you might have on others.

It is important to know your personal strengths so they can be better leveraged and cultivated. Also, acknowledging your personal development opportunities, whether they are behavioral or technical in nature, allows you to put plans and actions in place to enhance your current performance and impact, as well as realize your true potential for future performance success.

Areas to consider for enhanced self-awareness.

- Specialized / technical training
- Work / life experiences
- Unique skills / talents
- Team interactions
- Leadership style
- Behavioral traits
- Decision-making process
- Communication style
- Stress management
- Conflict resolution style

All of these areas require constant attention, development and feedback. Leverage your identified skills and tendencies that are strengths, and engage in development or change efforts to minimize your gaps or weaknesses.

As you build your foundation for performance success you should:

- Be keenly aware of your alignment to your organization.
- Understand that each of us is defined by our actions and judged by our reactions in all situations.
- Gain self-awareness for performance growth and success.

In the following section we build upon this foundation by creating a solid framework of personal and team development actions and activities.

FRAMEWORK

As we look to build on and leverage the firm foundation of enhanced organizational, situational, and self-awareness, our attention turns to creating a solid personal development framework.

You can create a very targeted and powerful personal plan for growth and development by focusing attention and planning on the three key areas for performance enhancement: eligibility, suitability, and viability.

01	02	03
FIRST KEY AREA	SECOND KEY AREA	THIRD KEY AREA
ELIGIBILITY	SUITABILITY	VIABILITY
Required job and technical skills	Natural behavioral traits and characteristics matched to position	The actual impact of an individual's eligibility and suitability

Performance results and your current and future potential are more than just what you do today. They also comprise what you can do, how you do it, and the natural talents you possess. When combined, your eligibility, suitability, and viability will provide you with clarity, alignment, and accountability for any development activities and plans you might create and share with those you impact and who impact you.

Eligibility

The developmental framework begins with eligibility. Whether you have aspirations for career advancement or are focused on career enhancement, it is important to advance your eligibility. Eligibility consists of the knowledge, skills, past performance, experience and credentials required to perform and fulfill the requirements of your current or future role. By building your eligibility, capability and capacity you enhance your overall impact, influence, technical performance, and ensure your ongoing relevancy.

As we look to the future of organizational performance, identifying your unique talents, in addition to your training, education and job knowledge, and then applying those talents to unique organizational and functional opportunities, will maximize your impact and personal job satisfaction.

In the past, most performance reviews focused mainly on this part of the framework, your eligibility, with a heavy emphasis on discussing past performance. While this discussion is certainly important to have, it is only a small portion of a complete and effective leading performance plan.

Key areas for eligibility planning:

If your goal is advancement:

- Identify the future role job description and requirements, and take a

personal inventory of your current skills, knowledge, and training eligibility, as well as any gaps that might exist.
- Develop a plan for leveraging current eligibility and identify the resources, actions, activities and relationships required to close any eligibility gaps.

If your goal is enhancement:

- Gain feedback on your current performance from leaders, peers and subordinates (if in a leadership role).
- From the feedback, identify areas of strength to leverage and cultivate opportunities for personal improvement.
- Develop a plan that will continually enhance your relevancy, team and personal impact, and current eligibility.

Suitability

As mentioned earlier, in past performance models eligibility was nearly 100 percent of the focus. However, as you establish a more effective and comprehensive blueprint for performance success, it is just as important, if not more so, to continually reflect on and cultivate your behavioral suitability. This is an inventory of your behaviors, traits, tendencies, and work preferences; essentially, how you get your work accomplished. This is where you are defined by your behaviors and actions and, rightfully or not, judged by your reactions and the daily impact those reactions have on your work relationships and activities.

While so much focus has been on reviewing your eligibility and past performance, remember, 80 to 85 percent of a person's success or failure is actually behavioral. You can have all the technical talent in the world and be able to deliver results, but if your attitude and behaviors or your ability to connect with people is lacking, those results will almost certainly be marginalized.

Often behaviors that contribute to success at certain levels of the organization and in specific roles might actually be a hindrance at other levels or in other roles. With your leader or mentor, proactively discuss the critical enabling behaviors in any role you are currently performing or aspiring to perform, and identify those behaviors that might lessen your impact and success.

Viability

Your development framework is almost set. The next step is to enhance your viability. This is the true measure of the value of your contribution to your organization and team. Viability is the actual observation and experience that others have of your actions, attitudes and values, and the results you consistently exhibit and deliver. It is the combination of what you do (eligibility) and how you do it (suitability). It equates to how well you do what you do and the overall impact and value you provide.

Think of it as: **Eligibility + Suitability = Viability**

To gain awareness to your viability, continually ask peers, leaders, subordinates or others who might have regular and meaningful interactions with you to provide you with development feedback. Think of it as a continuous 360 assessment. We can think of this immediate and continuous feedback as Uber-driven performance. Think about it, an Uber driver receives a performance review after every ride. That review is up for public viewing and often determines if others are going to pay for that driver's services. Too many two-star reviews and the driver is out of business! What if individuals you interacted with in meetings, on phone calls, in presentations, or just around the office rated you after each personal experience with you? How long would you stay in business?

Are you delivering the desired results and impact in alignment with your department's and organization's purpose, vision, mission, and values on a consistent basis?

Viability requires being open and honest with yourself, as well as asking others for objective feedback about the value you provide and how well you provide that value.

QUICK REVIEW

This is a lot of information, so let's quickly recap what we have covered so far in our blueprint for individual performance.

We have discussed the importance of forming a firm foundation for personal performance growth by establishing greater organizational-, situational-, and self-awareness. We have built on that foundation a development framework that defines actions, activities, and development planning that increases your eligibility and suitability, which in turn creates greater, and more effective personal viability.

ENHANCEMENT

The final component of the blueprint for performance is the continual focus on enhancing your skills, abilities, behaviors and impact. Truly setting your performance value up for success requires a next-level commitment of time, effort and focus on continual growth and enhancement. It is not just thinking about today, but identifying and cultivating your future potential. Engaging in planning and activities to achieve that future potential will only increase your value and relevance in your organization.

Potential

In most organizations, at the beginning of the year there is often talk about succession planning and developing the people within the organization. Many organizations have, at some level, invested time and money in a high-potential development program. Organizations do it, but do you? Are you focused on identifying and developing your personal potential? When asked, most individuals cannot clearly identify or articulate their current or future potential. What do you aspire to achieve? Where are you in that pursuit? What can you do to start moving toward your own aspirations?

As humans, we are designed for improvement and if we stop aspiring and developing, we fall into comfort zones and become complacent. With the pace of change around us continually accelerating we can quickly lose our value and relevance.

Do not let this happen. Create an action plan with resources. Resources can include things such as technology, people, financial resources, training and physical resources that will help you realize your potential. Make sure you have clarity and alignment with your leader or mentor on the potential you have identified before putting the resources in place. This is an extremely important part of your blueprint. Work each day to reach your potential and to deliver outstanding performance.

Impact

And what is the true performance differentiator? Impact. People engage in work and all the activities associated with work, but what is their true impact? I am sure most of us have been associated with people who get a lot of work done, but because of the attitude and behaviors displayed in getting that work accomplished have an immensely negative impact in the workplace. We call this the "Island of Negativity".

NARRATIVE CASE STUDY

The boss at Antero, an internet technology firm, just released new company-wide guidelines for productivity. Dan cannot stand it. He thinks the company is just fine the way it is. Dan goes over to Jeremy and says "Can you believe the boss's new guidelines? They're awful!" Jeremy responds, "I know they're horrible! This company is headed in the wrong direction!" Dan just got Jeremy on his island and it grew just a little bigger. He is feeling good so he now goes over to Jan, another person who always agrees with him. "Can you believe the boss? He doesn't have a clue what he's doing!" and Jan comments back, "I know. I agree. Ugh, it's the worst!" And now Dan has Jeremy and Jan on his island. Soon enough, the whole department is on Negativity Island and the performance culture has become toxic.

But there is hope for changing the tide and shrinking it back to a lonely, isolated island! Let us see the same scenario played out in a different way.

The boss releases the guidelines. Dan heads on over to Jeremy and says, "Can you believe the boss's new guidelines? They're awful!" This time Jeremy responds with, "I know, it's rough, but what can we do to make it better and help him out?" This is not what Dan was expecting and his island shrinks a little. But Dan's not worried, he knows that Jan is always on his side. "Hey Jan! Can you believe the boss? He doesn't have a clue!" However, Jan says, "Yeah, I know, but I'm tired of being negative. What are we going to do to provide some help with this?" Dan is now alone on his tiny Negativity Island and the department's performance culture can thrive. Dan will either be forced to change or leave the company because the company has now become toxic for Dan.

CREATING A MORE PRODUCTIVE OUTCOME

You can make an impact on those around you just by intervening in a positive and supportive way and by reframing and refocusing on success, resulting in a more productive outcome.

In addition, you can make a positive impact by acknowledging and recognizing the efforts of others around you. Just a sincere thank you or an acknowledgement of their efforts can go a long way to making a difference in the workplace. For example, what about those professionals in your IT organization who get very little credit for all the systems up time and get all the blame for those few times the system goes down. Just a quick thank you to those individuals can have a major impact.

So while performance is important, your overall impact is what truly counts. The opportunity for you to deliver results, and make a positive impact in doing so, is an incredibly powerful performance duo.

With a foundation, a framework and enhancements in place, your blueprint for performance success is now set to enhance your relevance, value and viability. However, the most critical component in moving from having your performance managed and reviewed to enabling and pursuing your performance, is to lead where you are. Step up and create an effective and sustainable performance feedback environment that you own and lead. We call this the performance connection.

PERFORMANCE CONNECTIONS

The old performance management model of the manager setting goals, establishing expectations and giving semi- and or annual performance reviews with little or no feedback along the way is an ineffective performance model, and it has been for over 40 years. It is your performance and your career, and now it is time to take control of it. It is time to flip the performance model. True performance is all about clarity, alignment, action and feedback. We do this by establishing and leading ongoing performance connections with our managers.

Truly sustaining that next level of performance success in this complex and ever-changing business environment requires ongoing performance connections, not just once or twice a year review cycles.

These connections are employee led, not manager led, and consist of 15 to 20 minute conversations, held every four to six weeks. They establish an ongoing dialogue of feedback focused on performance clarity, alignment and accountability, with a goal of mutually agreed upon performance expectations.

After having a performance connection, you should be able to clearly articulate:

- New Expectations
- Expectation Accomplishments
- Expectation Challenges
- Opportunities to Accelerate or Change
- Barriers to Success
- What's Next

If you invest time in conducting these performance connections consistently and frequently there should be no surprises at the end of the year. You gain and provide clarity along the way and you ensure that you stay aligned and connected on your performance. In the end, you and your leader should leave with greater performance clarity, complete alignment, clear accountability on your commitments, and an understanding of what to expect and the future desired impact.

If your performance, for any reason, is lacking or you are struggling, it is better to acknowledge and confront it rather than make excuses, blame, justify or ignore it. Adjust your blueprint and get back on track. If necessary, make your connection meeting a weekly occurrence to provide you the greatest opportunity for success and to show that you are doing everything in your power and control to deliver on your promised results. Even when times get tough or you get "too busy," don not stop making these connections.

Remember, if you follow your performance blueprint and use these performance connections, by the end of the year there will be no need for managing performance. You will have been enabling and leading your performance all year long.

LEADING PERFORMANCE ACTION ITEMS

Gain organizational awareness by seeking clarity and alignment to the organization purpose, mission, values and priorities.

Develop your situational awareness by acknowledging and understanding the impact your natural actions and reactions have on situational outcomes.

Have greater impact on your personal performance results by being aware of your strengths and areas for development. These can be both technical and professional traits and attributes.

Focus on developing your three key performance dimensions of eligibility, suitability and viability.

Invest time each month in defining, refining and cultivating your potential and sharing your progress with those who support you.

Set aside time each month for your performance connections to gain insights and a progress report on your performance. No end of year surprises!

It truly is your performance, your career, now in your control.

Step up and lead your performance!

3

Leading Relationships

"The most important single ingredient in the formula of success is knowing how to get along with people." — Theodore Roosevelt

"I am convinced that nothing we do is more important than hiring and developing people. At the end of the day you bet on people, not on strategies." — Larry Bossidy

---

Imagine you are an Executive Assistant in 1995 and your boss has just asked you to organize an executive meeting between five separate locations and departments for about 20 managers. You get to work and grab your Rolodex. For those that do not know what a Rolodex is, it is a physical rotating file device used to store business contact information. You start flipping through it and begin calling each of the other Executive Assistants to determine the schedules of their respective managers.

An hour later, you have made your calls and discovered that only half can make the initial scheduled time for the meeting, but have additional times for each of the managers that would work. After another 45 minutes, you have narrowed it down to a time that would work for all managers. Now you call each one of the Executive Assistants back to confirm the new time. Unfortunately, five of the managers now have a department meeting scheduled during that time. Back to the scheduling board. Another 30 minutes later and you have found another time that should, fingers crossed, work for all managers. You call all Executive Assistants back again and finally, success! And it only took four hours of your time to schedule one meeting.

An exaggerated story, but still a valid example of how far we have come in the communications arena. It is incredible to see how developing, cultivating, maintaining and leveraging personal relationships, even something as simple as scheduling a meeting, have changed so drastically in just the past two decades. Unfortunately, the ease of communicating is also replacing the fine art of relating.

CONNECTING VERSUS COMMUNICATING

Each of us receives hundreds, if not thousands, of emails, marketing ads, texts messages and other forms of communication each day. Additionally, did you know that the average person speaks over 16,000 words per day? All of this adds up to a whole lot of communicating with potentially little or no relationship being established.

This ability for us to communicate anywhere, 24/7, whether we like it or not, is the new normal no matter your age, gender, work culture or position in work or life. If we are not careful, we can easily lose the art and practice of developing relationships. We cannot just rely on communicating, we must also make sure to connect.

In this chapter, we will explore three key types of business relationships and how we can lead our way back to developing and maintaining impactful connections with others, moving past the "bits and bytes" of communicating to actually building something lasting. With that said, all relationships are not created equal! With little time to devote to cultivating relationships, it is important to recognize the differences and the strengths and pitfalls of each type of relationship.

And finally, it is important to understand and cultivate your sphere of influence. The sphere of influence is your visual representation of all your day to day relationships. Seeing and understanding your sphere is the cornerstone to leading and maintaining your move from communicating to truly connecting.

PROPERLY INVESTING YOUR TIME

Let us begin by defining "relationship". Depending on which dictionary you grab or website you navigate to, they will all give you something to the tune of "Noun. The way in which two or more concepts, objects, or people are connected, or the state of being connected." In today's fast-paced and complex world, the time available to establish and cultivate relationships is near zero. To effectively lead and influence where we are, we must get back to developing and, more importantly, investing in authentic, personal relationships each day.

As stated before, not all relationships are created equal, so not every interaction will be an investment in authenticity. However, it is important to develop your personal awareness and skill set for identifying the interactions that require a proactive investment from those which are more transient and transactional in nature and impact. With limited time, and that limited time ever-fleeting, we obviously cannot invest the same time and effort in every relationship. Think back on your interactions with others over the past day, week and month and you will likely see a startling pattern. It is highly likely that 80 percent of your impact and value has come from only 20 percent of the relationships and interactions you engage with in a given timeframe. Yes, that's correct, only 20 percent of your relationships will account for an overwhelming percentage of your personal impact and effectiveness! We call these our Critical 20. This is precisely why it is so imperative that we know how and where to spend our relationship investment efforts.

THE THREE TYPES OF RELATIONSHIPS

As mentioned, there are three key relationship types we encounter: transient, transactional and authentic. Each relationship will be one of these types; however, relationships can change, so just because one is initially labeled transient does not mean that over time it will permanently remain there. And actually, as we begin to lead and cultivate our relationships, we can purposefully transform them based on our desired impact.

TRANSIENT RELATIONSHIPS

Transient - Lasting only for a shirt period of time, impermanent.

With the advent and popularity of social media and new technologies, transient relationships have become more prevalent than ever and that number only grows. They have exploded with our endless capabilities to "connect" with hundreds or thousands of "friends" and acquaintances through Facebook, Twitter, LinkedIn, text messaging, and so on.

While all these tools for staying connected are important for how we live, interact and succeed on a daily basis, there is a large difference between "staying connected" and actually connecting with other individuals. They allow for near-instant communication and quicker response times; however, they can easily become distractions and unknowingly become barriers to truly connecting. If not used with care, they can become a way to avoid important and sometimes difficult situations as we try to handle them virtually, which leads to disengagement and negative impacts both personally and professionally. We must be vigilant while establishing and using these transient connections.

Good uses for transient connections include information gathering, making initial contact and reestablishing past connections.

Again, we must be careful when using and analyzing transient relationships as they can easily be mistaken for something more meaningful than they are. As we all should know, not everything posted on the internet is true. These types of relationships certainly have their place in our lives and work environments, but we cannot let them take away the valuable time we need to cultivate and establish our Critical 20.

The Strengths of Transient Relationships

- Ease of contacting a large number of people
- Searching for individuals from the past
- Connecting with people that have mutual interests or roles
- Making an initial contact point

The Possible Pitfalls of Transient Relationships

- Potential to become a distraction and time-waster
- Easy to mistake for a deeper level of relationship
- Difficult to determine how real or genuine is the connection
- Little or no commitment or accountability for actions or words

TRANSACTIONAL RELATIONSHIPS

Transactional - Communication or interaction involving two or more individuals that impacts those involved or others.

Transactional relationships are the most common type of business relationship you will have and will likely account for over 80 percent of your business relationships. The sending of emails or texts, conducting phone calls, or in-person interactions where the outcome of the interaction is most important, not the relationship itself, is the true definition of a transactional relationship. The most important aspect of the interaction is the transaction with no further time or effort given to cultivating a deeper understanding of the person, situation or information beyond the value given and received from the transaction.

Obviously, being an integral relationship type in any business, and sometimes personal setting, it is important to ensure you gain the most from each transactional relationship. This can be achieved by mutually defining success (early and often) on what the outcome of the transaction should be, and identifying the who, what and how required to achieve that outcome. Creating that anchor point of mutually agreed upon success and discussing roles and expectations of all parties involved enhances the chances of staying focused and achieving success, even when barriers arise. Mutually defined success gives each party a fall-back point for quick alignment and realignment without wasting precious time and resources.

Keys to effective transactional relationships:

- Mutually define success
- Agree on roles and responsibilities
- Set expectations and stay aligned to those expectations
- Remain flexible
- Admit mistakes and accept responsibility for outcomes

Having a "no matter what" mentality in each transactional relationship will enhance personal accountability and help ensure the transaction's success. Each individual must lead the effort and take personal responsibility for all outcomes, no matter what!

AUTHENTIC RELATIONSHIPS

Authentic - Worthy of acceptance or belief, as conforming to or based on fact. True to one's own personality, spirit, or character. Sincere and authentic with no pretensions.

While 80 percent of our relationships are of the transactional nature, our Critical 20 are our most coveted. As stated at the beginning of this chapter, this 20 percent will produce up to 80 percent of value in most business and personal environments.

The Critical 20 are special relationships that require us to develop, cultivate and invest time and resources in them to create deeper, more authentic relationships. However, our ability to communicate instantaneously and continuously can sometimes stymie the art of connecting authentically. "Bits and bytes" have begun replacing real, genuine, interpersonal relationships.

When asked to describe authentic relationships people often state words like "real," "genuine," "true." So how do you create these real, genuine, true relationships? You must take the time and make the effort to invest in that relationship. Get to know that individual. Get out of your world and into theirs. Bottom line, you have to have the intention to cultivate authentic relationships.

Review your personal sphere of influence and identify your current Critical 20. Are these relationships authentic, transactional or transient? The majority of these, if not all, should be authentic. If you are not sure, it is easy to do a quick authenticity check. Just ask yourself these questions about each person:

- Do you know what they value?
- Do you know what they expect?
- Do you know what they want?
- Do you know how they like to work?
- Do you know what barriers or obstacles they may be facing?
- Can you mutually define success for your relationship?
- Do you know them on a more personal basis, and can you work through disagreements amicably?

An authentic relationship will have you answering yes to the majority of these questions.

Developing these relationships requires the commitment of time and effort. It takes the willingness to move from "What do I get out of this?" to "What can we accomplish together?" Asking, "How can I help?" and "What's possible?" can transform a relationship from mediocrity to a highly productive, "results together" relationship. This type of relationship is simple and yet complex at the same time. It takes a concerted effort to ask, not tell, and to actively listen, hear and understand.

You know the relationship is authentic when:

- Trust is established and continually shown
- Mutual success is defined and aligned
- You can count on that person no matter the circumstances
- You hear and say, "How can I help?"
- You get out of your daily world and into theirs for a deeper understanding and connection
- Relationship and outcomes are equally important

The Strengths of Authentic Relationships

- They stand the test of time and adversity.
- There is enhanced accountability by all parties.
- They eliminate blame, justification, and excuses.

The Possible Pitfalls of Authentic Relationships

- Ongoing time must be invested in developing and cultivating these relationships or authentic will migrate to transactional.
- You should assess whether the targeted relationship and impact of that relationship warrants the significant time required to develop it.

Having a better overall understanding and awareness of the relationship types, we can now lead and cultivate relationships more effectively. With so many distractions and time-wasters competing for your attention, knowing where and how to invest time and resources in your relationships is critical.

SPHERE OF INFLUENCE

The final step in leading relationships is putting it all into practice. For this, we must gain clarity of our relationships using what is called our Sphere of Influence. Gaining this clarity will help with identification and development of our relationships.

Each and every one of us has a unique Sphere of Influence. Think back over the past few weeks to all the emails, calls, text messages and voicemails you have sent and received. Now, think about all the social media interactions you might have had as well. Within these contacts are the people who comprise your Sphere of Influence. A list of these interactions, properly analyzed, can be a highly effective tool for leading your relationships. The goal of analyzing and sorting these relationships is to discover who make up your Critical 20 and then to answer these three questions:

- What am I going to do to make sure my Critical 20 are effective, authentic relationships?
- How will I invest my time ensuring my transactional relationships are the most impactful they can be?
- What is my transient relationship strategy to ensure my time is well spent?

A good goal to set is to update your Sphere of Influence each quarter. As the pace of business, projects and personal priorities changes, so do our relationship needs and focus. Leading relationships takes time, energy, and a carefully thought out plan to most effectively cultivate and sustain our business and personal relationships. Make sure to stay focused on your Critical 20 and how you and those individuals can make the most impact.

LEADING RELATIONSHIPS ACTION ITEMS

Strive to create connection with others, not just communication.

Limit time invested in transient relationships and use it sparingly to reconnect or initiate contact.

Make sure to mutually define success in your transactional relationships and ensure roles or activities are aligned and clear.

Invest time cultivating meaningful relationships with your Critical 20. Understand not just the transactional roles and activities, but understand the needs, wants and challenges in the relationship.

Identify and continually update your Sphere of Influence as projects and priorities, both personal and professional, change.

4

Leading With Purpose

"To begin to think with purpose, is to enter the ranks of those strong ones who only recognize failure as one of the pathways to attainment." — James Allen

"If you can tune into your purpose and really align with it, setting goals so that your vision is an expression of that purpose, then life flows more easily." — Jack Canfield

"Efforts and courage are not enough without purpose and direction." — John F. Kennedy

It should come as no surprise that creating a sense of purpose in our work as well as in our personal lives leads to greater engagement in whatever it is we choose to do. This added engagement leads to better performance, enhanced productivity and generally higher levels of satisfaction in what you do. Study after study produces these outcomes and yet for some reason we still tend to focus and strive to complete tasks for numbers (profits) or tangible things that tend to wear us down and wear us out.

These tasks are usually put down as goals, and goals can certainly be helpful in achieving certain things, but not when it is to the detriment of our own success! We tend to get so caught up checking off our task lists that we end up forgetting why we were checking them off in the first place. And that is where we begin, the "why."

In the 1960s, President Kennedy was visiting NASA. While on a tour he saw a man walking down the hallway with a broom and a bucket. President Kennedy walked over to him, introduced himself and said, "What do you do here at NASA?" The man, who was clearly a janitor, replied, "Mr. President, sir, I am helping to put a man on the moon." Now that is connecting to higher level purpose!

MATCHING TALENT TO OPPORTUNITY

Creating a sense of purpose starts by connecting what you do to the impact you are having. Martin Luther King Jr. said it best. "If it falls your lot to be a street sweeper, go out and sweep streets like Michelangelo painted pictures. Sweep streets like Handel and Beethoven composed music. Sweep streets like Shakespeare wrote poetry. Sweep streets so well that all the hosts of heaven and earth will have to pause and say, here lived a great street sweeper who swept his job well."

Our ability to match our talents with our opportunities and to create a lasting impact on our customers, co-workers and family energizes us and in return energizes those around us. Purpose inspires and it rouses us to be better today than we were yesterday and better tomorrow than we are today.

PURPOSE IN THE WORKPLACE

Let us start with purpose in the workplace. Why is it important for the organization to create a sense of purpose when their employees arrive at work? The answer to that question comes with a fairly simple answer: it creates a greater sense of accomplishment and self-worth for employees by giving meaning to the tasks they are being asked to do and pursue. By providing that meaning, the organization not only inspires their current employees but also begins to attract more committed and engaged employees who have a thirst for meaningful work. All of this strengthens the workplace performance environment, leading to greater innovation, more diversity, and delivering top-tier results.

TASK-FOCUSED TO PURPOSE-DRIVEN

But describing why creating purpose is important is the easy part. Shifting the organization performance environment from task-focused to purpose-driven requires a large commitment and asks the leadership to do much more than just focusing on the bottom line. Change is never easy, but it usually comes with a few benefits, and this change is no different.

What is the difference between a task and a purpose? Here is one simple question to ask that can bring it into focus: Do I wake up each day with a purpose to achieve a task, or is my task to wake up each day to achieve a purpose?

Take a look at the following chart. Evaluate what you do on a daily basis and then ask yourself those questions again.

Task-Focused ⟩ Purpose-Driven

Information
The task-focused individual's only goal is to gather information and do what has been told to do regarding the information.

Insight
A purpose-driven individual takes information and turns it into insights gaining a greater intuitive understanding of the what, how and why regarding the information.

Activity
A task-focused individual focuses on only the activity itself. The activity is seen as a «check the box» activity and just needs to be completed, nothing more.

Impact
The purpose-driven individual sees the task or activity as a chance to make a true difference. The activity is just the launching point to other possibilities and real impact.

Compliance
This individual just complies. The manager says what needs to be done and how it should be done and there is no thought to the impact or process. It just gets done.

Engagement
True engagement is what being purpose-driven is all about. This individual is thoroughly in-tune personally and organizationally and is constantly pushing the envelope to make things better.

These are two very different situations with two very different outcomes.

Creating a new emphasis on purpose, in addition to profits, has shown to generate short-term confidence and greater long-term success. The shift in focus grows organizational confidence and drives growth according to a 2014 Deloitte study on the Culture of Purpose.

THE PROFIT CAN TAKE CARE OF ITSELF

These organizations, both new and old, have truly embraced the concept of purpose and it has taken them to the top of their respective industries.

Disney – Disney is not just in the business of creating TV shows and movies, building and distributing toys, and running the most successful theme park system in the world. While those are things they do and create, Disney's entire point of being in business, as stated by them, is to "Create Happiness."

Facebook – Whether you like or dislike, agree or disagree, with Facebook, it is one of the largest media companies in the world, and they have a reason for doing what they do. Mark Zuckerburg has stated that Facebook exists to "Give people the power to build community and bring the world closer together." This statement of purpose creates the foundation for successful innovation and has built an empire in a relatively short period of time.

And last, **Recreational Equipment, Inc.**, better known as REI, has created one of the most well-known and successful outdoor lifestyle brands in the United States. Their task of selling clothing and equipment and running global adventure vacations are just what they do, but REI's stated reason for doing it all is to "Inspire, educate, and outfit for a lifetime of outdoor adventure and stewardship."

These companies are constantly on "Great Places to Work" lists, and the purpose or meaning they give their employees for the work they do is a large reason for those achievements. You see, with a heavy focus on purpose, the profit often follows.

WHAT IS PURPOSE?

What exactly is purpose? Well, the official definition states: "The reason for which something is done or created, or for which something exists."

Simple and direct, and it gives us an excellent framework for our deeper, more authentic definition: Purpose is the driving force behind creating or doing something of which the result is impactful to not just the business, but also its employees, customers, and community.

But is this the type of rhetoric we typically see on the walls or websites of organizations? For sure, most companies have some version of a mission statement and a vision statement, and these are important to have, but most companies and individuals confuse one or both of these statements with the purpose of the organization. Let us clarify.

> A **mission** is what we are doing. This describes what the organization or individual does and the intention.

> A **vision** describes the future successful state of the organization's or individual's goals.

> A **purpose** is why we do what we do. Outwardly focused, it provides meaning behind the product or service.

ACHIEVING A PURPOSE

With a better understanding of the differences in these company statements, what is the key to achieving purpose within an organization?

The only way purpose can ever be truly achieved is by ensuring two things: clarity and alignment.

This might seem obvious, but to gain clarity it is initially important to define what the organization's overall purpose is, followed by each department's or team's purpose.

Once the purpose is defined, the next step in gaining clarity is to understand how you and your co-workers relate to that purpose and how it motivates you. Understanding this should give you good insight into how your purpose fits into the organization's or team's purpose.

Once clarity has been achieved, alignment to that purpose needs to be gained. Take the organization's purpose and your personal stated purpose within the organization. How do they match up? Are they closely aligned? Or do gaps exist? If gaps do exist, here is where you can formulate a plan to gain increased alignment and close those gaps.

A LITTLE PERSPECTIVE

But what happens if there is a lack of purpose within your organization? What do you do to create individual purpose in that type of environment? Become engaged in your organization. Be intentional and get involved. Think about what gives you meaning both at work and in your personal life. Ask for clarity from those close to you and your manager or leader and encourage your organization to make its purpose known. This will make aligning your purpose much easier.

While hurdles and barriers do and will exist, creating individual purpose in the absence of organizational purpose begins with just thinking about things a little differently. Understanding that simple acts, such as holding the elevator for someone or grabbing papers off the printer for a co-worker can have a purpose. Instead of doing it just because it is the right thing to do, do it because you want to help that person out. Go grab some fresh air not because you feel stressed, but because you like the way the open air and sun feels. Sometimes purpose just needs a little perspective.

CREATING INDIVIDUAL PURPOSE

Finding and creating purpose also does not have to be a complex, earth shattering idea. Keep it simple, but meaningful. Your purpose in a single day can be as simple as leaving your workplace better than when you walked in. Complimenting someone else's work, offering constructive advice, even picking up a piece of trash that was left in a hallway are all ways you can achieve that purpose.

Most importantly, get more in touch with what drives you from day to day. What energizes you? Is it connecting with others? Contributing to a team? Organizing company events? Whatever it is that energizes you, focus on doing more of that.

Unfortunately, organizations and managers may not always provide you with a clear-cut purpose within the organization's framework. The organization may not even know what their purpose is, but that should not stop you from finding and creating your own purpose each and every day. Make it your task to achieve a purpose each day!

LEADING WITH PURPOSE ACTION ITEMS

Putting an emphasis on purpose has shown to generate short-term confidence and greater long-term success.

Each day ask yourself, "Am I more task-focused or purpose-driven?"

Gain clarity and alignment around your personal purpose within the organization and the organization's purpose.

Become engaged in your organization, be intentional, and get involved with the culture.

5

Leading Accountability

"Leaders inspire accountability through their ability to accept responsibility before they place blame." — Courtney Lynch

"Responsibility equals accountability equals ownership. And a sense of ownership is the most powerful weapon a team or organization can have." — Pat Summitt

---

Have you ever been in a meeting where a productive discussion suddenly turned to blaming and justifying, making excuses and fingers being pointed? Or have you ever received personal feedback that surprised you? You've been working overtime, delivering what you've felt are on-time, quality results only to find out others are saying you can't be counted on? Most, if not all of us, have had experiences similar to one or both scenarios during our careers.

Leading where you are is the essence of showing personal accountability. The true measure of accountability resides not in how accountable you view yourself (we would all say we are accountable), but in the views of those with whom you interact and work with on a daily basis. Would they say, without a doubt, that you are accountable?

Millions of dollars and thousands of hours are invested in trying to train people to be more accountable and on training managers to hold their people more accountable. The problem with this model is that accountability is not a skill that can be trained and sustained. Accountability is individual and team actions and behaviors that are consistently shown over time.

This gap between individuals thinking they are accountable and organizations as a whole rating low in accountability exists in nearly every organization. We know this from the results of employee engagement surveys we have conducted. Invariably, one of the focal areas for change is accountability. So why does this gap exist? It exists because we are conditioned to it. Individually, everyone thinks they are accountable, but, that is not the true measure. The true measure is whether *others* think we are accountable. That disconnect is what produces the gap. We call this the Accountability Gap.

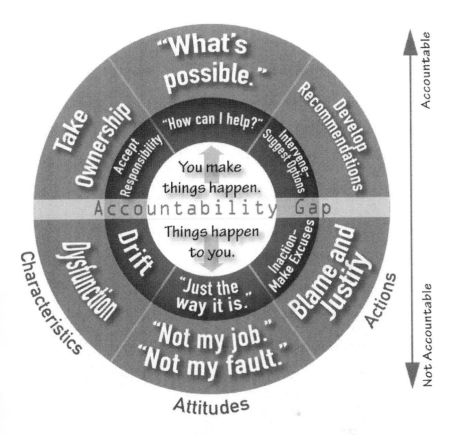

Accountability Continuum

The Accountability Continuum shows that, when below the line, things are just happening to you. Drift and dysfunction are clearly apparent, people are saying statements like, "That's just the way it is." and blame and justification is the standard reaction in tough situations. Crossing above the Accountability Gap means you move from having things happen to you, to making things happen. You take ownership and responsibility, saying things like "How can I help?" and "What's possible?" and you start suggesting options and developing recommendations instead of just placing blame. A negative performance environment is never allowed to adversely impact your behavior and results.

So how do we shift an environment of blame, justification, drift, and excuses? You do so by leading where you are, proactively controlling what you can, making things happen, and accepting responsibility and accountability, no matter what! Yes, that's right, no matter what — even if senior leadership, your manager, or your peers lack accountability.

FROM THOUGHT TO ACTION - LEAD WHERE YOU ARE

To continually bridge the Accountability Gap, all individuals must recognize and acknowledge their personal responsibility to be accountable, no matter what. We are responsible for always growing and developing ourselves, as well as those around us.

When we do not accept that responsibility and leave it up to others, we tend to become victims of circumstance. And victims of our own making at that. Things happen to us instead of us making things happen. We cannot force others to be accountable, as hard as it is to admit, and we have no control over how accountable others actually are or are not. But we do have complete control over how accountable we ourselves are and we have the obligation as we are leading where we are to help and develop others to hold themselves accountable.

Leading accountability is taking all the chapters you have just read and beginning to lead where you are.

If you are leading change by seeing possibilities in everything, thinking disruptively without acting disruptively, and creating options and recommendations for change, then you are leading with personal accountability.

If you own your performance by proactively setting performance expectations with your manager, setting time each month on their calendar to review your performance and owning your results, then you are exhibiting personal accountability. You do not let negativity adversely impact you or those around you. I you ask "How I can I help?" and you intervene if and when drift in your organization happens, then you are leading with accountability.

If you are leading relationships by developing and cultivating more authentic relationships, promoting a positive performance environment by your actions and activities and you follow-up and find ways to add value in all you do, then you are leading with accountability.

As we have already learned, accountability begins and ends with taking a good look at what we do and how we act (and react) on a daily basis. It is important to make a concerted effort to hold ourselves accountable to the actions, commitments and behaviors that exhibit role model and individual leadership, whether you are in a formal leadership position or not. It starts and feels small initially, but accountability breeds success. By truly committing yourself to being accountable and leading where you are, others will follow suit and the environment of accountability around you will grow.

NARRATIVE CASE STUDY

On June 2, 2010, Armando Galarraga, a major league baseball pitcher for the Detroit Tigers was one out away from being the 21st pitcher in history to throw a perfect game (no opposing player reaches base in the game). With two outs in the ninth inning, the opposing batter hit a ground ball to the first baseman who then tossed the ball back to Galarraga who came over from the pitcher's mound to cover the base. The immediate reaction was one of jubilation from the Detroit Tigers only to quickly find out that the first base umpire, Jim Joyce, had called the runner safe. Video review in the park, on the television, and after the game clearly showed Galarraga and the ball had beaten the runner to the bag and the runner should've been called out, preserving the perfect game. Keep this in mind, this was before instant replay was installed and challenges allowed. The call was "Safe!". Devastating for a pitcher to experience. Galarraga, nonetheless, marched back over to the mound, without throwing a fit, and finished the game by getting the next batter out. A one-hit complete game shut-out win, but a perfect game robbed.

However, in an unusual and rare move, umpire Jim Joyce tracked down Galarraga and the media after the game, and with tears in his eyes, apologized for the blown call. Yes, you read that right, an umpire apologized for the blown call. Talk about being accountable for your actions.

To finish the story, Galarraga forgave Jim Joyce stating, "He probably feels more bad than me. Nobody's perfect. Everybody's human. I understand. I give the guy a lot of credit for saying, 'I need to talk to you.' You don't see an umpire tell you that after a game. I gave him a hug." So, you have a pitcher who was just robbed of something special show forgiveness, and a major league umpire admit his mistake and show true accountability.

THE FOUR A's TO ACCOUNTABILITY

To help in the journey towards true, role-model accountability, we developed the Four A's to Accountability, a four-step process that gives us a path to follow to becoming accountable.

Accept

Accept the responsibility of flipping a "blame and justification" environment to one that offers recommendations. Reframe conversations by asking questions such as "How can I help?" or "What can we do to improve this situation?" Accept the fact that you may be the only individual accepting responsibility and accountability and that you will not fall victim to circumstances when others are not being accountable. Accept the responsibility for intervening when projects or meetings begin to drift and that you may have to act as the leader even though you may not be the formal leader. And accept that things may not always go according to plan. Be flexible and adapt as situations and scenarios change.

Act

Accountability is action. Doing nothing is a choice, but it rarely leads to success. Sitting back and just letting things happen is the ultimate failure of not being accountable. Act by defining your role and responsibilities. Clearly define what success means, and establish clear milestones. Follow up on progress with individuals and teams, give credit more often than you take credit, and create options and recommendations. Do not place blame or make excuses.

And remember, act, do not react. Keep your actions and reactions consistent and positive. You are defined by your actions, but you are judged by your reactions!

Adjust

Your ability to adjust to different and changing circumstances will help to create a successful environment. We do not have control over all circumstances, but we do have control over how we adjust to each circumstance. As circumstances change, so must we. If barriers or obstacles exist, adjust your thinking and plans along the way. Keep an open mind to new options and perspectives.

Adjust your style when needed. If dealing with differences in communication or decision-making styles, learn to adapt.

Adjust your attitude. There are times when we have to occasionally take a step back and reassess situations through a new lens or from a different angle. Do not waste time getting mired in frustration when success is likely right around the corner. Refocus and recommit. Be persistent, but flexible; success is often more about tenacity than genius.

Achieve

Work to achieve one milestone, one action, one adjustment at a time! Do not get overwhelmed and do not take on too much.

Continually give updates on progress, and personally reward and recognize others, giving credit to others while taking little for yourself. Use these tools to establish your personal record of accountability and the momentum and inevitable success that follows will become unstoppable. Accountability breeds success.

LEADING ACCOUNTABILITY ACTION ITEMS

Lead Where You Are – Lead change (see chapter 1), lead your performance (see chapter 2), lead with relationships (see chapter 3), and lead with purpose (see chapter four).

Where blame, justification and excuses reside, reframe the discussion by redefining success and ask "How can I help?"

When things begin to drift, accept responsibility to do something. Create positive and future-focused discussions and action planning.

Put negativity on an island! Don't fall victim to negativism and offer support by focusing on what can be done, not dwelling on the past or what is wrong.

Define success and continually align to that success.

If management provides no direction or confusing priorities, accept responsibility to seek clarity by opening a positive dialogue about your current understanding of expectations and gain alignment from there.

6

Conclusion

At the start of this book we asked if you were ready? Are you ready to step up and step in to lead where you are? It is our hope that this book has given you the tools to thrive in today's new and exciting performance environment.

Even if your organization is slow to evolve or never evolves, you can, at the very least, invest in yourself. It is your performance and your career in your control. Leading where you are cultivates a personal brand that has a positive impact on others and your organization.

Now, when faced with barriers and obstacles, you should see possibilities for change, making things happen and not just waiting for them to happen. You think disruptively, while not acting disruptively, in a world of disruptive change. You create options and recommendations, act with urgency, and never stop leading change.

By leading your performance, you own your performance: good, bad or indifferent. You set the expectations for your success and activities to achieve that success with your manager. You set time aside each month to review your performance, allowing you and your leader to focus on pursuing performance rather than waiting for the traditional annual end-of-year performance review conducted by your manager. No more

CONCLUSION

surprises!

You know the value of developing and cultivating authentic relationships, not hiding behind "bits and bytes" communication. You have defined your sphere of influence, and identified your transient and transactional relationships. You have relationship plans for your Critical 20, but most importantly, you continually invest in and value all your relationships.

You have identified and aligned your work purpose. You come into work with a task to contribute to your purpose, not with a purpose to complete a list of tasks.

By leading where you are you begin leading with accountability and are accountable no matter what, even in the absence of accountability. You accept the responsibility to act in a positive way when you see blame and justification occurring or are faced with those negative individuals that seem to exist in every organization.

You adjust to dynamic situations, knowing that while we do not have control over all circumstances, we do have control over how we react and adjust to those circumstances.

You are now ready to go out and lead where you are, and make a positive difference each and every day!

LEAD WHERE YOU ARE
ONLINE PACKAGE

The world is more complex, the opportunities are more dynamic, and performance leadership is shifting from top down to enterprise wide. To compete and thrive, each of us must lead where we are, no matter where we are. Cultivating the leader in you requires continual learning, active development, and ongoing reinforcement. Invest time in developing these as core competencies by completing all Lead Where You Are courses!

40% off with code
ebook2020

ONLINE PACKAGE DESCRIPTION

In this online course package, you will continue to focus on the five Lead Where You Are competencies contained in the ebook, taking what you learned and formulating action plans to turn those insights into increased impact.

The Lead Where You Are Package includes all five (5) interactive courses, guidebooks and resources.

Plus receive a free Lead Where You Are Trait Assessment (reg. $15)!

SIGN UP TODAY!

WWW.CORNERSTONELEARNING.COM/PROGRAMS

PERFORMANCE ADVISING

Our model for enhancing performance is different.

Cornerstone Learning provides an integrated approach to enhancing performance. Our focus is enhancing both the individual leader and their team's connection and performance. Focusing the coaching on just the leader misses the opportunity for exponential performance impact. Leveraging over 25 years of our experience and insights, we have developed a performance enhancement model that extends our impact beyond traditional "executive" coaching programs and tools. Our advising model raises the bar of individual, team and organizational performance.

Gaining Insight (1)
We set the foundation by helping to mutually define success between the participant and the leader, gaining team and organizational perception and performance feedback and begin to level-set team engagement, alignment and impact.

Creating Awareness (2)
Once the foundation is set, we focus on identifying current performance strengths and gaps, identifying behavioral traits that contribute to performance success and traits that potentially derail success. This helps to develop a realistic understanding of performance potential.

Developing Success (3)
We then turn that awareness into defined developmental actions and activities, create a targeted personal and team enagagement plan and conduct a team alignment and performance development session.

Ensuring Accountability (4)
To ensure ongoing accountability we establish a sustainable and dynamic performance development plan, invest in and enable ongoing team enagagement and development activities and create the foundation for ongoing performance connection sessions with your leaders.

Cultivating and Sustaining Team Engagement (5)
Traditional performance coaching is good but incomplete without focused attention on enhancing team engagement and performance as well. Cornerstone Learning's performance advising engages the leader and their team to clarify team purpose, cultivates team engagement and provides the reinforcement tools and framework that elevates both individual and team performance, closing the gap that can often exists after traditional one-on-one coaching.

LET US SHOW YOU A PATH TO SUSTAINABLE SUCCESS.

WATCH OUR PERFORMANCE ADVISING VIDEO AT
WWW.CORNERSTONELEARNING.COM/ADVISING

About Cornerstone Learning

Our purpose is simple. To enable your success. At Cornerstone Learning we believe sustained success is achieved through building employee-engaged, leader supported and organization enabled performance environments. And this is how we're different. We are not a "one size fits all" training program. Each client engagement is unique because each organization is unique in its challenges, current level of performance engagement and vision for success. We create and enable applied learning environments that work on real-time opportunities delivering real-time results. Learning and development are achieved by doing. We partner to transform traditional, passive performance management into dynamic performance pursuit and enablement. We create performance legacies, not corporate training programs or initiatives pushed down through an organization. Our role evolves as results and success are achieved. And we ensure sustainability through immersion, engagement and reinforcement. Come see how we can enable your success.

Visit us at www.cornerstonelearning.com.

Subscribe to our newsletter:

✉ https://www.cornerstonelearning.com/lead-where-you-are-signup

Made in the USA
Columbia, SC
29 November 2021